P9-DWS-630

SUMMITS AND STARLIGHT

SUMMITS AND STARLIGHT

THE CANADIAN ROCKIES

Photography by Paul Zizka
Foreword by Glen Boles

This book is dedicated to my loving wife, Meghan, who has been incredibly supportive of my passion over the years, and my newly born daughter, Mistaya, whom I am very much looking forward to introducing to all the joys of the mountains in the years to come.

FOREWORD

The world's great mountain ranges such as the Alps, Himalayas, Andes and the Saint Elias Mountains, are well known because they have been the subject of many books with great pictures that show off their overpowering size. However, the Canadian Rockies, while they can't claim the same extreme elevations, take a back seat to none, especially when it comes to scenery, mainly because of the beautiful lakes, rivers and mountains that dot the landscape along the Continental Divide between Alberta and British Columbia. Over the years, the two photographers who stand out and have left their mark on the history and scenery of the Rockies—more than any others—are Byron Harmon and Bruno Engler.

With the arrival of digital cameras, as well as the multitude of wide-angle and extreme telephoto lenses available today, there are many young photographers who are making *their* mark by taking spectacular mountain photos to new heights. One such photographer is Paul Zizka, whose photos fill the pages of this very elegant book. Today's photographer has an edge over the photographer of the past. They can shoot many frames, then easily cancel the ones they dislike. In the past, you had to perform this procedure in the darkroom.

Aside from climbers, skiers, hikers and other members of mountain communities, most Canadians know very little about our mountains. Most books on the subject feature photographs of the same areas over and over, usually taken from the highway. This book, with its spellbinding photos taken from unexpected vantage points, will hopefully encourage both young and old to appreciate our mountains, and will pique the interest of the local mountain community with unique views of the mountain areas they have not had the opportunity to visit.

The story of how I met Paul is quite interesting. For several years, my wife Liz had wanted to spend a night at the Num-Ti-Jah Lodge, located on the shores of beautiful Bow Lake, in Banff National Park. So, in 2007, for her sixty-fifth birthday, I booked us in for the night of June 23. When we checked in after we had been for a hike with some friends, we were advised that someone had left me a message requesting a meeting. I didn't recognize the name, but I agreed to meet this person in the lobby after supper. When we sat down for supper that night, it turned out that the young man who had left me the message was also our waiter: Paul Zizka. He was a dashing, good-looking guy who wanted to talk to me about climbing mountains. So Liz and I invited him to have breakfast with us the following morning. We spent an interesting time talking to this sincere and impressive young gentleman about mountains. After that initial encounter, we were to meet up with Paul in the Banff area more and more often.

It is interesting to note that when Paul started taking photos, cameras that use film were on the way out, so all of his pictures were taken with his digital cameras. In some ways, our pictures are quite different: I was working on climbers' guidebooks and I wanted to take many of my photos in crystal clear weather so that the climbing routes could be seen clearly in the photographs.

That is not to say I did not take pictures under varied circumstances and conditions, but, like Paul, I was passionate—even fanatical about the adventure of seeing new areas and photographing them. On this point, I am sure we share the same feeling. On the other hand, Paul specializes in photos taken in adverse conditions so that the viewer can see how extreme the weather can be and what the mountains can serve up when you are out and about under bitter weather.

Paul's pictures are individualistic, distinctive, unique and different. His favourite locations to photograph are the heavily glaciated areas along the Continental Divide. Many of his pictures are taken during challenging conditions, which he clearly thrives on. This is the reason they stand out and portray the myriad unexpected faces of the mountain environment so beautifully. Sit back, relax and enjoy the book.

Glen Boles

PREFACE

The twenty-first century can be hard on the adventurous spirit, calling us to greater creativity as we look for new ways to explore the world around us. From peaks yet unclimbed to remote corners yet untouched, it is easy for one to feel that "everything has been done." There's a question my mountaineering partners and I often ask ourselves, typically over dinner at an Alpine Club of Canada hut, or as we read the oldest entries in a seldom-visited summit register: I wonder what it would have been like to arrive in the Rockies during the golden age of exploration, along with the likes of Outram, Schäffer, McArthur, Feuz or Collie? What an exciting time that would have been! Could we have contributed, in some tiny way, to opening up those new areas and routes in these wild places we have grown to love? Could we have been the first to set eyes on a particular mountain or glacier?

I used to feel like I was born one hundred years too late, but photography has taught me that mountain exploration has no end. My fascination with mountain environments has much to do with the ever-changing interplay of light and weather one finds among these rugged lands. I find that this dynamism allows for a new visual experience with each visit. As J. Monroe Thorington so eloquently wrote, "We were not pioneers ourselves, but we journeyed over old trails that were new to us, and with hearts open. Who shall distinguish?" Nowhere in the world is this more evident than in the mountains. For me it is photography that keeps my "heart open," by asking me to pay attention.

Summits and Starlight is a collection of what I feel are my finest, most compelling Canadian Rockies images from the last five years, a collection that offers a fresh photographic perspective of our Shining Mountains. A small portion of the images were taken during the classic "golden hour" at iconic roadside locations that many people will recognize. Most photographs in the collection, however, took a considerable amount of work to capture, whether they were taken deep in the backcountry, at high elevations during mountaineering expeditions, or during the darkest hours of the night under star-filled skies. Many were taken under light or weather conditions perhaps not traditionally associated with landscape photography. As such, I hope that this book will reveal a side of the Canadian Rockies many people have yet to experience and that these pages will evoke in the reader a desire to preserve this unique part of our planet for generations to come.

May these photographs inspire you to dream, keep your heart open and seek adventure into the wild.

Paul Zizka
March 10, 2013

ACKNOWLEDGEMENTS

My utmost gratitude goes to the Bow Valley community for their ongoing support of my photographic efforts, with a particular shout-out to the local photo community. I feel fortunate to live alongside many talented photographers who inspire me on a daily basis.

I am also very thankful for the multiple opportunities I have had to work with Banff Lake Louise Tourism and Parks Canada in promoting our stunning part of the world.

Thank you also to all those who preceded me on the trails and put so much effort into exploring, documenting and preserving these special places. In that regard I am particularly thankful to Glen and Liz Boles, Rick Collier, and to Chic Scott.

I also owe a million thanks to my friends and partners in adventure who so willingly (or not) froze their digits off for photographic purposes, kept me safe in the mountains and who appear in this book: Meghan Ward, Ian Luckhurst, Dave Paynter, Adam Zier-Vogel, Fabian Roberts, Quentin Roberts, Makyla Walerickton, Lukas Prochazka, Rachel Slater, Valérie Trudel, David de Courville, Laurel Carlton, Greg Dineen, Venessa Langhorn, Kevin Mager, Ross Sabourin, Lindsay Hill, Mike Stuart and Doug Urquhart. Thanks as well to Max Elliott, Shannon Sabourin, Lee and Becky O'Donnell and Jen Judd for their ongoing support of my work, and to everyone who has shown interest in my photography over the years. Nothing has gone unnoticed.

A sincere thanks to the great team at Rocky Mountain Books, including Don Gorman, Chyla Cardinal, Joe Wilderson, Neil Wedin and Melanie Rutledge, who made this book possible and gave me a lot of freedom in putting it together.

To the Ward family, your ongoing encouragement has meant the world to me. A mountain-sized thank you to my family, particularly to my parents, Claire and Jacques, and to my brother Étienne, who have always offered their unconditional support and love.

Finally, my gratitude goes to my own little family. First, to my newly born daughter, Mistaya: I just can't wait to see the mountains through your eyes. And of course to my wife, Meghan, who truly shares my passion for the mountains, has sacrificed a lot to make this book happen and has been an unwavering source of support and inspiration to me since the beginning.

INTRODUCTION

There is nothing like crossing a glacier in an electrical storm to remind you who is in charge—not that the day to that point had been free of challenges. The incessant downpours of June 2012 had left the Niles Meadows trail in shambles, and much of it lay underwater. Carrying the overnight packs up 1200 metres and over unstable snow to Niles Col had left everyone a little weary. Trying to beat approaching tenebrous clouds to the top of Mount Daly to sneak in a rushed ascent had made matters a little worse. And when the first drops of freezing rain hit shortly after we set foot on the Waputik Icefield, I think we all understood that the last kilometre to the Scott Duncan Hut was going to be the most demanding. As lightning flashed all around, the sound of thunder grew closer and our axes started to buzz. When the rain turned from pouring to torrential and the visibility dwindled, I was thankful we were going to stay at the alpine hut that night.

My idea was to head to a location that was elevated and largely free from light pollution. A coronal mass ejection—a major solar event—was going to disrupt the Earth's magnetic field that night and produce perhaps one of the decade's finest displays of aurora borealis. The Scott Duncan Hut seemed to fit the bill, and my wife, Meghan, and friend Ian were keen to head up there with me. The thought of watching the northern lights dance for hours over the Waputik Icefield, and being able to photograph them from the vicinity of a warm, dry shelter, appealed to me tremendously. Except that when we finally got to the hut, soaked from head to toe, the winds were howling and the rain was travelling sideways. Our hopes of seeing the aurora that night had all but vanished.

It amazes me that after twelve years of wandering in the mountains I still underestimate how quickly Mother Nature can turn things around. My slumber was soon interrupted when the alarm rang at ten o'clock. I reluctantly crawled out of my sleeping bag and dragged my feet toward the hut door, expecting to be greeted by whiteout conditions and back in the arms of Morpheus in no time. But in that moment the magic of the mountains struck yet again, further cementing my passion for the hills. As I opened the door I could clearly see emerald ribbons of aurora gracing the northern horizon, even though darkness was just settling in.

I will never forget the hours that followed. I woke up my companions and then scoured the bouldery, snowy slopes surrounding the hut in my down booties in search of aesthetic compositions. Amazingly, both sides of the Continental Divide remained shrouded in clouds. Yet, right above our little, improbable shelter, the skies stayed clear for several hours, giving us a window into one of the best celestial shows we had ever witnessed at such latitudes. In the silent night, the vast expanse of the Waputik Icefield faithfully reflected the colours and patterns overhead.

As a photographer, I was overwhelmed, but did my best to document the event and what it felt like to be there. But most of all, I just felt thankful. Thankful for what these mountains have added to my life. Thankful for the sanctity of these alpine lands. Thankful for a lifetime of mountain moments ahead.

See page 33 to view an image from that night on the Waputik Icefield.

THE JOURNEY WEST

Like many who dwell in the mountains, I spent the first few years of my life in the flatlands of eastern Canada, more or less unaware that the rest of the world was much different. Growing up in Quebec City, but having relatives living up in the Lac Saint-Jean area, we would regularly drive across the Laurentian Mountains for family visits. Seeing the ancient, heavily eroded roots of the Grenville Belt—which, I excitedly found out several years later, had been, at one point, possibly one of the highest mountain ranges in the history of our planet—was my first exposure to topographical relief. Even though the Laurentians are rounded, forested and barely reach 1000 metres in elevation, their presence planted a seed. I recall gazing out the car window and wondering which bump was the highest, and whether there were higher bumps hidden behind.

In 1996 I stood among the Canadian Rockies for the first time. Two companions and I did what all the easterners do on their first visit to the big mountains: We hitchhiked up to Banff, dipped our feet in Moraine Lake, took a few photos of elk with our disposable cameras, braved the fences at the Athabasca Glacier and, having nowhere to sleep, unrolled our sleeping bags by the mailboxes at Lake Louise's Samson Mall. It was only a brief stay and I don't recall being particularly fascinated by the Rockies at that point, but I believe this whirlwind visit contributed to a growing spirit of adventure and a gradual appreciation for mountain environments.

In 2000 I was back in Banff National Park. This time I would be staying the summer and working at red-roofed Num-Ti-Jah Lodge on the shores of Bow Lake. That summer shines as one of the pivotal moments of my life, and if I were asked when I fell in love with the mountains, I would immediately think back to that time.

Living a distant forty kilometres from Lake Louise with no car to access it, and with countless possibilities for outdoor pursuits right at my doorstep, I started to explore. Almost daily, I sought adventure in one way or another. Back then, I'd hit the trail in cotton clothing, carrying very little, thanks to my rather limited awareness of mountain hazards. Many times I recall running down rocky slopes, known as scree, and getting back to the lodge a few minutes before my shift in the dining room—just enough time to jump in the shower and show up to serve my first table.

Like many ambitious twenty-one-year-old easterners, I dodged the odd bullet. On my very first scramble up Observation Peak, I misjudged how hard the snow surface would be in the cold, wind-whipped 3000-metre air. I slipped and tumbled down the summit slopes for what felt like an eternity. Thankfully, I was back at the lodge uninjured and on time for work.

I spent seven blissful summers at Bow Lake, meeting like-minded folks, nurturing my relationship with the mountains and developing my capabilities in the alpine environment. At first, I spent the other parts of those years studying geology at the University of Victoria. Summertime meant climbing mountains, while the winters were made tolerable by learning how those peaks came to be, what they are made of and how they evolve. Later on, freedom from school allowed my mountain exploration to take on an international dimension. Days after finishing my degree, I set off on a solo, unsupported 1400-kilometre double crossing of Iceland, which remains one of the formative experiences of my life. That trip would be one of many to mountainous or volcanic destinations around the globe in the years to come: Ethiopia, Norway, Svalbard, New Zealand, the South Pacific, Nepal, Alaska, Yukon, Nunavut and the contiguous United States of America.

Toward the end of my time at Num-Ti-Jah Lodge, I met my wife, Meghan. As we walked up Cirque Peak, explored ice caves by the Bow Glacier and camped on Mount Jimmy Simpson, we discovered a shared passion for the outdoors and talked excitedly about the adventures calling our names. When our final season at the lodge came to an end, we spent a month backpacking in the Caribbean and made the decision to return to the Rockies. This time, we longed to be part of a community larger than the one we'd previously enjoyed at Bow Lake, and the Town of Banff became the obvious option.

In the spring of 2008 we arrived in town with nothing but our bags. We had no jobs, no accommodation—only a fondness for mountainous places and a commitment to giving Banff a trial year. We returned to the hospitality industry as a temporary way to make ends meet, turning every weekend into a long weekend of hiking, climbing or ski touring. Gradually, we found a way to combine our outdoor passions with our professions. Keen to spend as much time outside as possible, I started guiding and registered a photography business with the town, while Meghan focused on outdoor, travel and adventure writing.

One year turned into two, then three, then four. By our fifth year it was obvious the mountains had a tether on our hearts and wouldn't let go. We could now call this mountain town "home" and welcomed our daughter, Mistaya, into the world on March 22, 2013.

A MOMENT IN TIME

Photography for me simply started as a rather dry and somewhat selfish way of documenting remarkable places, light and weather events. I have a practical mind, and picking up a camera seemed to be the obvious way of chronicling the mountain experience. With time, I became increasingly fascinated with the interplay of light, weather and the landscape and this expanded my emotional connection to high places. While my other mountain activities brought me into the landscape in a special way, I realized that photography allowed me to observe nature more closely. Looking at the wilderness through the camera lens made me more aware of my surroundings, and my observations became more deliberate. I began paying attention to how sunlight filtered through the evergreens, how all but one twig pointed in the same direction, and how fast the clouds were moving. Soon this magnified way of observing the natural environment became indistinguishable from living life as I had known it.

I also realized that with enough intention, a photograph has the power to affect people who weren't there when it was taken and who had no previous history with the location. The ability to freeze a moment in time, and the challenge of conveying the meaning of that moment to others, remains a very appealing part of photography for me. It amazes me how very different types of wild spaces can stir up similar emotions in folks living on opposite sides of the world; how, as photographers, we have the potential to make an impact on others through an arrangement of colours and shapes, and how a single frame can come incredibly close to letting someone experience snow or the aurora in some meaningful way, without actually being there in person to witness these phenomena.

Growing up in suburbia, but having lived in close proximity to mountain wilderness for years now, it has become increasingly apparent to me that humans have become disconnected from the natural environment, from where we originated eons ago. We have, essentially, walked away from nature. From this emerges a new sense of purpose for me: the possibility to invite people to go back to the wilderness through my images and to be reminded of what the natural world adds to one's life. I have no doubt that reconnecting with nature is a big part of solving our common world issues. And by extension, I feel I can play a role in preserving these special places so that this crucial connection will remain strong for generations to come.

INSPIRATION AND APPROACH

Oddly, it is not the work of other photographers that inspired me to pick up a camera. That interest came later as I got curious about how fellow artists went about documenting their own experiences, and as I developed a fascination for remote places, particularly the backcountry of the Canadian Rockies.

I find tremendous inspiration in the work

of those who travelled through these mountains well before me. Beyond photography, I draw plenty of inspiration from the early mountaineers of the Canadian Rockies: the likes of James Outram, Conrad Kain and Christian Kaufmann. I find it unfathomable when I contemplate how much these pioneers accomplished given the odds they faced back then, let alone their antiquated gear.

In terms of photographic influences, I have found the dedication and passion of pioneers Frank Hurley and Vittorio Sella to be admirable and their work, utterly fascinating. Here in the Rockies the images of Byron Harmon and Bruno Engler keep me observing and exploring, and regularly stoke my desire to document the magic of our wild places. The black and white work of Craig Richards reminds me to pay attention. Finally, the work of Glen Boles epitomizes not only what life in the mountains means to me, but has also inspired my personal approach to photography. In his work I discover a deep respect for the mountain environment, a keen eye for artistry and composition, and a spirit of exploration and adventure.

Mountain photography, especially in the backcountry and on mountaineering exploits, bears many challenges. For one, getting to locations may require considerable physical effort. Mountain weather can also be at times harsh on one's gear, as well as on the photographer, both physically and psychologically. In the mountains, Mother Nature is unpredictable and can repeatedly deceive the bewildered photographer. The mountain environment also brings strictly technical challenges: the inadequacy of graduated filters due to rugged skylines, the ubiquity of high-contrast scenes owing to the presence of snow, and the difficulty in conveying a sense of scale in a place where everything is so immense.

The technical challenges involved in mountain photography aside, I have never been a gear junkie and have never been overly interested in photographic equipment. I consider what's in the bag to be tools, sitting there alongside my harness or ice axe. I invest in quality gear to ensure I capture the highest-quality images, but beyond that, my passion is invested in what lies beyond the lens and not the lens itself. I've smashed enough lenses in my time to learn not to get too attached.

For all the reasons listed above, I believe that beyond skills, fitness and gear, one needs to have an adaptable approach in order to capture magical moments in our part of the world. As a consequence, a limited amount of planning goes into my photographs. I may head to a particular location at a time when I feel conditions will make for fine images, but everything else is decided on the spot. You will never hear me say, "This shot has been six months in the making, waiting for the right conditions to come together." Most of the time I prefer to work with what I'm given.

My approach to photography can be divided into two parts. The first part consists of simply being aware and going about one's day with an image-maker's perspective, or eye. Other artists will relate if I refer to a "second brain" that constantly analyzes from a photographic standpoint. Each scene is examined for its potential as a photograph. This happens routinely, somewhat passively in the background, whether I am in the wilderness, running errands on Banff Avenue, or on holiday in some exotic location. Of course, it helps to be able to drop everything and pick up the camera if I consider the conditions to be suitable to photography. I am very thankful for the people around me who allow me my moments of spontaneity by the roadside, on trails or high up in the mountains.

The second part of my approach is determined on the scene and in the moment: background, foreground, lens, aperture, duration of exposure, and more. I believe the fickle nature of the mountain landscape, light and weather lend themselves better to this type of spontaneous photography. Of course, it helps to be very familiar with the mountains, but dynamic conditions call for a dynamic approach.

This way of working also allows one to be more in tune with the ever-changing environment and to appreciate the multitude of moods found in the Canadian Rockies landscape. Accepting that conditions may not always come together for a compelling image, and being able to enjoy my surroundings even if it means coming home without satisfactory photographs, are both important aspects of my approach. Things will quickly get frustrating for a photographer who is set on getting a specific image but is unable to enjoy a grey sky or a few raindrops. This is particularly true when photographing remote or hard-to-reach places, where one just does not have the luxury of returning to a location easily or frequently.

Moreover, what is for me the limiting factor in terms of what makes a strong image—composition—typically only comes together in the short term. I know that with enough persistence and time spent out in nature that the interplay of light, weather and a given subject will eventually work in my favour and lead to what I feel is a compelling result.

A CASE FOR THE ROCKIES

Having spent time in Patagonia and Nunavut, I know that the Canadian Rockies, or at least their protected areas, are not quite as wild as some other ranges. A few days spent in Nepal and the Andes makes it obvious that size is not what sets the Rockies apart. They do not have the geothermal spectacles of Icelandic Highlands nor the oceanside drama of Alaskan peaks.

But with time I have become increasingly aware of how special the Canadian Rockies are among all the other mountainous places of the world. The one thing that makes these mountains stand out as photographically unparalleled is how everything comes together. The diversity is remarkable, and this includes, of course, the weather. It is truly amazing how many moods Mother Nature can display within a twenty-four-hour period. Add to that the fact that the Rockies have four distinct seasons, and each one holds its own unique combination of elements.

The high latitude has other advantages: the occasional aurora borealis; the glorious winter sidelight; the many glaciers, which in turn dot the landscape with world-famous turquoise lakes in the summer. What is more, geology has left much more to photograph than chiselled peaks: caves, hoodoos, teetering towers, serrated ridges, boulder fields, fossils, waterfalls and an array of spectacular sedimentary rock features. Don't forget the myriad wildflowers in the summertime, the ever-present wildlife, the chinook and lenticular clouds and the star-filled skies at night. To add more interest to it all, toss in a rich layer of human history dating back thousands of years.

Just like the scenery, access to that scenery is also a fine blend. These Canadian Rockies have the perfect mix of accessible and remote landscape photography opportunities. One has the ability to create dramatic landscape photographs directly from the roadsides. But it is also still possible to wander around the backcountry photographing for days without seeing a soul, even in the height of summer. The opportunities for exploration and creativity are endless.

Hence, from a photographer's point of view, the diversity is astounding, setting the Canadian Rockies apart as the "jack of all trades" of mountain regions. But it's how all this diversity comes together in the right proportions that makes it seem divinely orchestrated. Whenever I get the chance to explore other mountain regions of our planet and allow myself to compare with the Canadian Rockies, I unmistakably reach this conclusion.

SUMMITS AND STARLIGHT

BLAZING SKIES,
AURORA BOREALIS OVER LAKE MINNEWANKA,
BANFF NATIONAL PARK

VERMILION SILHOUETTES, MOUNT RUNDLE FROM VERMILION LAKES, BANFF NATIONAL PARK

ALL SHADES OF BLUE, LAKE O'HARA (LEFT) AND LAKE MCARTHUR (RIGHT)
AS SEEN FROM MOUNT ODARAY, YOHO NATIONAL PARK

EARLY SNOWFALL,
FIRST OCTOBER LIGHT ON CROWFOOT MOUNTAIN AND BOW PEAK,
BOW LAKE, BANFF NATIONAL PARK

CELEBRATION,
BOW LAKE,
BANFF NATIONAL PARK

BURNING MAN,
WAPUTIK ICEFIELD,
YOHO NATIONAL PARK

CATCHING THE LAST RAYS, MORAINE LAKE AND MOUNT TEMPLE FROM THE SUMMIT OF MOUNT BOWLEN, KOOTENAY AND BANFF NATIONAL PARKS

DOOR OF DREAMS, LYELL HUT OUTHOUSE, LYELL PEAKS

HEIGHT OF SUMMER,
MORAINE LAKE AND MOUNT FAY FROM EIFFEL PEAK,
BANFF NATIONAL PARK

ALPINE START,
GOODSIRS BASE CAMP,
YOHO NATIONAL PARK

DOCKSIDE SERENITY,
DOCK AT SPIRIT ISLAND,
MALIGNE LAKE,
JASPER NATIONAL PARK

AMONG GIANTS,
CHRISTIAN (LEFT) AND WALTER
PEAKS AS SEEN FROM THE
SUMMIT OF ERNEST PEAK,
LYELL PEAKS

QUIET MORNING,
BOW LAKE,
BANFF NATIONAL PARK

ALPINE GEOMETRY,
PARK MOUNTAIN,
YOHO NATIONAL PARK

PASTEL SUNSET,
LAKE MCARTHUR,
YOHO NATIONAL PARK

WATER SPIRITS,
LAKE MINNEWANKA
FROM THE AIR,
BANFF NATIONAL PARK

SAWBACK SPIRE,
MOUNT LOUIS,
BANFF NATIONAL PARK

INTERLUDE,
DUSK AT TWO JACK LAKE,
BANFF NATIONAL PARK

HANGING ON, NORTH FACE OF MOUNT TEMPLE, BANFF NATIONAL PARK

GLACIAL FLOW, CREVASSES ON THE ATHABASCA GLACIER, JASPER NATIONAL PARK

KNIFE-EDGE AFFAIR,
ROCK CLIMBING ON THE EAST-SOUTHEAST RIDGE OF MOUNT LADY MACDONALD, CANMORE

GREAT DIVIDE SUNSET,
JUNCTION OF YOHO, KOOTENAY AND BANFF NATIONAL PARKS

ON RAPPEL,
DELTAFORM MOUNTAIN,
KOOTENAY AND BANFF NATIONAL PARKS.
THE MIGHTY GOODSIRS ARE VISIBLE
ON THE RIGHT-HAND SIDE.

SAKNOWA STARS,

DELTAFORM MOUNTAIN,

KOOTENAY AND BANFF NATIONAL PARKS

TIGHT SQUEEZE.
THE FAMOUS CRACK PITCH ON THE MITRE,
BANFF NATIONAL PARK

MOUNTAIN-FLANKED SHORELINE,
FAIRHOLME RANGE AND LAKE MINNEWANKA,
BANFF NATIONAL PARK

MILKY WAY OVER RUNDLE,
TWO JACK LAKE,
BANFF NATIONAL PARK

FOCUSED.
CLIMBING ON THE MITRE,
BANFF NATIONAL PARK.

FIRST TO SEE THE SUN, SUMMER SOLSTICE HIGH UP ON MOUNT HECTOR, BANFF NATIONAL PARK

DAUNTING SIGHT, APPROACHING THE SOUTH RIDGE OF WALTER PEAK, YELL PEAKS

WONDER VALLEY,
MITELLA LAKE AND PROTECTION MOUNTAIN,
BANFF NATIONAL PARK

ICY BLISS,
ICE CLIMBING AT HAFFNER CREEK,
KOOTENAY NATIONAL PARK

SPRINGTIME SCRAMBLE,
MOUNT BALDY,
KANANASKIS COUNTRY

BLOCK LAKES SUNRISE,
BLOCK MOUNTAIN,
BANFF NATIONAL PARK

WINTER SPECTACLE,
GRIZZLY PEAK,
KANANASKIS COUNTRY

NO LINGERING,
POPES PEAK,
BANFF NATIONAL PARK

ERUPTION,
SUNRISE BEHIND MOUNT RUNDLE,
VERMILION LAKES,
BANFF NATIONAL PARK

REMOTE BEAUTY,
MOUNT WILLINGDON AND
UPPER MARTIN FALLS,
MARTIN VALLEY,
BANFF NATIONAL PARK

SCENIC LEAP,
STANLEY PEAK AND MOUNT BALL
FROM MOUNT WHYMPER,
KOOTENAY NATIONAL PARK

FORBIDDEN REACHES,
THE HEAVILY GLACIATED EAST
FACE OF MOUNT WILLINGDON,
BANFF NATIONAL PARK

SYLVAN SILHOUETTES,
TREES AT CASTLE JUNCTION,
BANFF NATIONAL PARK

OVERLAP OF SEASONS,
ASPENS AT HILLSDALE MEADOWS,
BANFF NATIONAL PARK

BATTLING THE ELEMENTS, A RAINY DAY OF CLIMBING AT TAKAKKAW FALLS, YOHO NATIONAL PARK

WINTER RIPPLES, BOW SUMMIT, BANFF NATIONAL PARK

SNOWBOUND,

SNOW PEAK,

BANFF NATIONAL PARK/KANANASKIS COUNTRY

AUTUMN ENCOUNTER,
HILLSDALE MEADOWS,
BANFF NATIONAL PARK

SILENT SPECTATORS,
AURORA BOREALIS OVER CASTLE MOUNTAIN,
BANFF NATIONAL PARK

AT ONE,
SELF-PORTRAIT AT LAKE MINNEWANKA,
BANFF NATIONAL PARK

LIMESTONE TILES,
CRUMBLY MOUNT CLINE,
DAVID THOMPSON COUNTRY

REEDS AND CIRRUS,
UPPER WATERFOWL LAKE,
BANFF NATIONAL PARK

PARADISE TRAVERSE,
TACKLING THE ROTTEN ROCK OF THE MITRE,
BANFF NATIONAL PARK

APOCALYPTIC SUNSET,
MOUNT RUNDLE AND TWO JACK LAKE,
BANFF NATIONAL PARK

UP THROUGH THE CLOUDS, SOUTHEAST FACE OF MOUNT ASSINIBOINE, MOUNT ASSINIBOINE PROVINCIAL PARK

PASSING THROUGH, CLIMBERS ON THE FAY GLACIER, BANFF NATIONAL PARK

UNFORGETTABLE,

SUNRISE ON MOUNT LITTLE,

BANFF AND KOOTENAY NATIONAL PARKS

MOONRISE AT ABBOT PASS HUT,
THE FAMOUS ALPINE CLUB OF CANADA HUT AT ABBOT PASS,
YOHO AND BANFF NATIONAL PARKS

THE MOUNTAINEER'S REWARD,
MOUNT VICTORIA,
BANFF AND YOHO NATIONAL PARKS

FALL PALETTE,
MOUNT FAIRVIEW, LAKE LOUISE,
BANFF NATIONAL PARK

APPARITIONS,
TREES AT VERMILION LAKES,
BANFF NATIONAL PARK

DWARFED,
KAYAKER ON ICEBERG LAKE
UNDER THE BOW GLACIER,
AT THE HEADWATERS
OF THE BOW RIVER,
BANFF NATIONAL PARK

HUMBLED,
SELF-PORTRAIT AT FLOE LAKE,
THE ROCKWALL LOOMING BEHIND,
KOOTENAY NATIONAL PARK

PRIDE OF YOHO,
LAKE O'HARA,
YOHO NATIONAL PARK

THE CRADLE OF MOUNTAINEERING, THE STATUE OF A SWISS GUIDE, FROSTED WITH SNOW, AT LAKE LOUISE, BANFF NATIONAL PARK

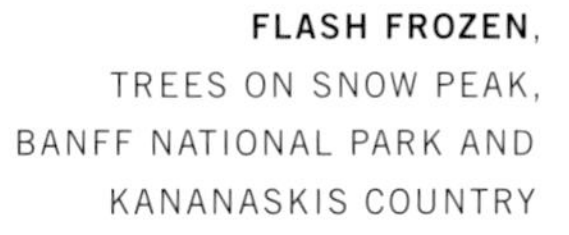

FLASH FROZEN, TREES ON SNOW PEAK, BANFF NATIONAL PARK AND KANANASKIS COUNTRY

MID-WINTER MAGIC,
SKI TOURING ON PEYTO LAKE,
BANFF NATIONAL PARK

EMERGENCE,
UPPER WATERFOWL LAKE,
BANFF NATIONAL PARK

SKY SURFING,
EMERALD PEAK,
YOHO NATIONAL PARK

DELICATE MOVES,
DOWNCLIMBING ON
MOUNT ASSINIBOINE,
MOUNT ASSINIBOINE
PROVINCIAL PARK

LIGHT ON SERACS,
ON THE NORTH TWIN,
COLUMBIA ICEFIELD,
JASPER NATIONAL PARK

MYSTERY ISLE,
ISLAND LAKE,
BANFF NATIONAL PARK

PRECIPICE,
MOUNT CLINE,
DAVID THOMPSON COUNTRY

NEW LIFE,
INDIAN PAINTBRUSH AT A PRESCRIBED
BURN NEAR MULESHOE,
BANFF NATIONAL PARK

WHERE SUMMER NEVER VENTURES,
A SNOWY ASCENT OF MOUNT SIR DOUGLAS,
KANANASKIS COUNTRY AND BANFF NATIONAL PARK

DIADEM ICEFALL,
NIGHTTIME OVER THE COLUMBIA ICEFIELD AREA,
DIADEM PEAK,
JASPER NATIONAL PARK

RESTING PLACE,
BIGHORN SHEEP REMAINS
ON PILOT MOUNTAIN,
BANFF NATIONAL PARK

MORAINE MOONLIGHT,
SUMMER NIGHT
AT MORAINE LAKE,
BANFF NATIONAL PARK

CELESTIAL SYMMETRY,
AURORA BOREALIS AT LAKE MINNEWANKA,
BANFF NATIONAL PARK

CAREFUL CLIMBING,
WHITE PYRAMID,
BANFF NATIONAL PARK

FEELING INSIGNIFICANT,
SKI TOURING ON THE
ROBERTSON GLACIER,
KANANASKIS COUNTRY

MOONLIT CONVERSATION,
SELF-PORTRAIT WITH CROWFOOT
MOUNTAIN AT BOW LAKE,
BANFF NATIONAL PARK

ILLUMINATION,
GOLDEN LARCHES
AT TAYLOR LAKE,
BANFF NATIONAL PARK

AUTUMN MORNING,
FLOE LAKE AND THE ROCKWALL,
KOOTENAY NATIONAL PARK

LUMINOUS LOUISE,
MILKY WAY OVER LAKE LOUISE,
BANFF NATIONAL PARK

THE SENTINEL,
GREAT HORNED OWL AND AURORA
BOREALIS AT LAKE MINNEWANKA,
BANFF NATIONAL PARK

ALPINE BLEAKNESS,
MOUNTAINEERS BELOW
MOUNT FAY,
AS SEEN FROM THE
SUMMIT OF MOUNT BABEL,
BANFF NATIONAL PARK

WHILE BANFF
IS SLEEPING,
AURORA BOREALIS OVER
VERMILION LAKES,
BANFF NATIONAL PARK

FIRST SNOW,
LAKE LOUISE,
BANFF NATIONAL PARK

THE RUNDLE SHOW,
MOUNT RUNDLE,
BANFF NATIONAL PARK

SWIRLING MISTS,
A LONE HIKER ON THE EAST
END OF MOUNT RUNDLE,
CANMORE AREA

ISOLATED,
SKI TOURING ON THE ICELINE TRAIL,
YOHO NATIONAL PARK

BASKING IN THE GLOW,
FIRST RAYS OF SUN ON DELTAFORM MOUNTAIN,
WITH NEPTUAK, HUNGABEE AND LEFROY
STANDING TALL IN THE BACKGROUND,
KOOTENAY AND BANFF NATIONAL PARK

CRYSTAL MORNING,
HOAR FROST ON TWO JACK LAKE,
BANFF NATIONAL PARK

MAGENTA MORNING, MOUNT BIRDWOOD, KANANASKIS COUNTRY

ENDLESS WINTER, SKI TOURING IN THE WATERFALL VALLEY,
ISOLATED PEAK AND MOUNT MCARTHUR FORMING THE BACKDROP, YOHO NATIONAL PARK

SPARKS OVER BANFF,
2012 GEMINIDS,
COMPOSITE IMAGE,
BANFF NATIONAL PARK

CHINOOK SKIES,
MOUNT RUNDLE,
BANFF NATIONAL PARK

STARDUST,
MILKY WAY OVER
CASCADE MOUNTAIN,
BANFF NATIONAL PARK

FRIGID FORTRESS,
CASTLE MOUNTAIN,
BANFF NATIONAL PARK

STARSTRUCK,
SELF-PORTRAIT AT LAKE MINNEWANKA,
BANFF NATIONAL PARK

TOWER OF MISTS,
EISENHOWER TOWER,
CASTLE MOUNTAIN,
BANFF NATIONAL PARK

EMERALD HORIZON,
AURORA BOREALIS
ABOVE MOUNT ASTLEY,
LAKE MINNEWANKA,
BANFF NATIONAL PARK

EUPHORIA,
FAIRY LAKE FROM
TROLLTINDER MOUNTAIN,
YOHO NATIONAL PARK

NIGHTTIME CANOPIES,
TREES AND THE NIGHT SKY AT MULESHOE,
BANFF NATIONAL PARK

SANCTUARY,
AURORA BOREALIS OVER PEYTO LAKE,
BANFF NATIONAL PARK

EDGE OF COLLAPSE, PORTAL PEAK AND WAPTA ICEFIELD, BANFF AND YOHO NATIONAL PARKS

GLOWING GIANT, SUNRISE BEHIND MOUNT HECTOR AS SEEN FROM BOW LAKE, BANFF NATIONAL PARK

HURRYING ALONG,
MOUNT BIDDLE, YOHO NATIONAL PARK.
SEVERAL LAKES ARE VISIBLE
IN THE BACKGROUND, INCLUDING
O'HARA, MCARTHUR AND MARY.

OLD FRIENDS,
A TREE LEANS TOWARDS
MOUNT INGLISMALDIE,
LAKE MINNEWANKA,
BANFF NATIONAL PARK

ABRAHAM BLUE,
METHANE BUBBLES AND
ELLIOT PEAK, ABRAHAM LAKE,
DAVID THOMPSON COUNTRY

RUNDLE AFIRE,
VERMILION LAKES,
BANFF NATIONAL PARK

STARLIGHT SPIRE,
SOUTH PEAK OF MOUNT EDITH,
BANFF NATIONAL PARK

THE DREAMER,
SELF-PORTRAIT AT LAKE LOUISE,
BANFF NATIONAL PARK

TECHNICAL NOTES

All of the images found in this book were captured with Canon 5D, 5D Mark II and 5D Mark III camera bodies, paired with EF 17–40mm f/4L, EF 24mm f/1.4L II and EF 70–200mm f/2.8L IS lenses. For a full list of gear visit zizka.ca.

DISCLAIMER REGARDING TENT IMAGES

For the camping image found on page 175, the tent was used solely for compositional purposes and the night was not spent on location. The photographs are not meant to suggest that it is acceptable to illegally camp within the boundaries of the mountain parks.

BIOGRAPHY

Paul Zizka is a professional mountain landscape and adventure photographer based in Banff, Alberta. Specializing in photographing in difficult conditions and hard-to-reach places, Paul has a passion for documenting the interplay of light and weather in the mountains, shooting alpine endeavours and unique international locations, and capturing the spirit of adventure. Paul's award-winning photos have been featured in a variety of publications, including *explore magazine, IMPACT* and *Canadian Geographic*. His commercial clients, such as Banff Lake Louise Tourism and Parks Canada, depend on his photography to bring Banff National Park to the world. See more of his work online at zizka.ca.

Rocky Mountain Books
www.rmbooks.com

Library and Archives Canada Cataloguing in Publication

Zizka, Paul
[Photographs. Selections]
Summits and starlight : the Canadian Rockies / Paul Zizka.

Issued in print and electronic formats.
ISBN 978-1-927330-92-0 (bound).— ISBN 978-1-927330-93-7 (html).—
ISBN 978-1-927330-94-4 (pdf)

1. Rocky Mountains, Canadian (B.C. and Alta.)—Pictorial works. 2. Photography of mountains—British Columbia.
3. Photography of mountains—Alberta. I. Title.

TR787.Z59 2013 779'.955143209711 C2013-903129-4
C2013-903130-8

Printed in China

Rocky Mountain Books acknowledges the financial support for its publishing program from the Government of Canada through the Canada Book Fund (CBF) and the Canada Council for the Arts, and from the province of British Columbia through the British Columbia Arts Council and the Book Publishing Tax Credit.

This book was produced using FSC®-certified, acid-free paper, processed chlorine free and printed with soya-based inks.